"Let the word go forth . . . that the torch has been passed to a new generation of Americans—born in this country, tempered by war, disciplined by a hard and bitter peace, proud of our ancient heritage—and unwilling to witness or permit the slow undoing of those human rights to which this nation has always been committed. . . ."

JOHN F. KENNEDY

THE
TROUBLE
IN
BERKELEY

The complete history, in text and pictures, of the great student rebellion against the "new university"

Text by Steven Warshaw

Picture editing by Mr. Warshaw and John W. Leahy, Jr.

diablo press

First Printing, April, 1965

Made in the United States of America

CONTENTS

PROLOGUE

In the fall of 1964, the University of California in Berkeley experienced a kind of trouble that hinted at problems infecting all American education. A group of its students rebelled against an administrative order limiting the content of their speech and advocacy, and they demanded that the University rid itself both of the order and of the personnel capable of issuing it.

In one respect, at least, the rebels, whose group was called the Free Speech Movement, were not disputed by the Administration: the University's simplicity was gone. One hundred years before the conflict two Congregational ministers, Sam Willey and Henry Durant, had started the school with 50 students. They paid a husband and wife $2.50 a week to run their campus, which contained a single building, and meanwhile they spelled each other teaching French, German, Latin, and Greek, and politicking for a state charter.

By the time of the rebellion the University was spread over nine campuses: regions each the size of a modern town, linked by a name, a ledger sheet in the state budget, and some administrators who used a small fleet of cars and airplanes to communicate with each other. In place of its first four administrators and scholars the University employed 40,000. Instead of the 100,000 Californians and the dying gold rush there were more than 18 million people and an economy in which it was necessary to waste materials in order to keep up with production.

The University no longer had to beg for the right to be involved with the state. The reverse was true. Its enrollment was over 72,000. It had to turn down thousands of applicants every semester. Its annual operating budget was more than one-half billion dollars; and its research grants, pouring out of government, foundations, business, and industry, ran to more than $175 million. In the beginning, the University got its Charter because one of its chief sponsors, Frederick F. Low, also became governor. Low remarked to Sam Willey, when the site of the Berkeley campus was being explored, "You have . . . scholarship, organization, enthusiasm, and reputation, but not money. We, in undertaking the state institution, have none of these things, but we have money. What a pity they could not be joined together." By the time of the rebellion they were inseparable. "The University," Clark Kerr, its president, said in defense of his Administration during the struggle, "is intertwined with all society."

Kerr thought that the changes at the University of California suggested a "new university" in the United States. He called it the "Multiversity."

This word, it turned out, had been used before Kerr by university presidents in Iowa and Minnesota. Kerr stressed it when delivering the Godkin Lectures at Harvard University in 1963, in the original draft of which, when prepared by his staff, it appeared as "multi-campus university." Thus a description of an intrinsically widespread university became one of a basically involved and complex one. In the whole drama that followed no other word, nor any act of Kerr's, so threatened individuality and therefore so provoked the rebels as "Multiversity." Kerr's book, *The Uses of the University* (Harvard University Press, 1963), which included the Godkin Lectures, amplified his thinking:

> *The current transformation will cover roughly the quarter century after World War II. The University is being called upon to educate previously unimagined numbers of students; to respond to the expanding claims of national service; to merge its activities with industry as never before; to adapt to and rechannel new intellectual currents. . . .*
>
> *The university has become a prime instrument of national purpose. This is new. This is the essence of the transformation now engulfing our universities.*

The sense of the Multiversity appeared to identify the University as part of the expanding web of power that is being developed in the name of automation, national defense, and research and development. This identification is what the University's rebellious students refused to accept. The students feared the power which the University was voluntarily supporting. Often when the national purpose seemed well defined by official policy, as in the American military involvement in Asia, they dissented from it. And they resented the increasing distance between their teachers and themselves. (In Berkeley, lectures are often given in auditoriums over microphones; tests are graded by teaching assistants, and there are so many final papers to be graded that the teaching assistants often subcontract them among fellow students.)

At the time of the conflict student idealism in Berkeley and elsewhere was being expressed within the larger struggle for minority rights in the United States. The spring and summer before, hundreds of Berkeley students affected major employers in Northern California, demanding, while chanting in marches and sit-ins, that Negroes be allowed equal job opportunities with whites. Hotels, restaurants, department stores, and automobile dealerships felt their anger, sensed their power, and surrendered at least some small part of prejudice. Many students went to the Southern United States to affect racial attitudes there through nonviolent action. They returned, after three students were tortured and murdered and others were whipped and beaten, with the psychology of soldiers home from an unfinished war.

Before the beginning of the new semester that fall, the 1964 Republican National Convention was held in the Cow Palace in neighboring San Francisco. The far right dominated Republican politics in 1964. Barry Goldwater, who became the inevitable Republican candidate after winning the California primary election during the previous summer, had taken positions which, if enforced from the Presidency, would have changed the basic direction of the civil rights struggle: the movement for Negro equality either would have been deflated or exploded into violence—probably the latter.

Students in Berkeley organized protests. They picketed the Cow Palace knowing, probably, that they were speaking more to the world than to the Republicans inside; for the Republican political commitments had been made and were irreversible.

Recruitment for the picketing of the Cow Palace took place in front of the Student Union Building on the University campus. There, students favoring causes traditionally set up folding tables on which they placed petitions, leaflets, and receptacles for contributions. The University permitted free speech on campus, but had not always done so. The past University president, Robert Gordon Sproul, had forbidden all political meetings in 1934, during the conflicts of the Depression, but the political climate had changed. The Administration's insistence that the staff sign a loyalty oath in 1949 had racked the faculty and, when liberal influence was restored, the oath had been modified. The ban on Communist speakers, imposed in 1951, was eliminated in 1963 under the pressure of litigation by students and the American Civil Liberties Union.

Soon after he became president in 1958, and again in 1961 and 1963, Clark Kerr issued a series of directives which codified the verbal understandings that the University had made with students on questions of free speech on the campus. Through the Kerr Directives he also interpreted this essential element of the University Charter: "The University shall be entirely independent of all political or sectarian influence and kept free therefrom in the appointment of its Regents and in the administration of its affairs." In Kerr's understanding, this meant that the "University and the name of the University must not be used to involve the University as an institution in the political, religious, and other controversial issues of the day."

University administrators expected that aloofness would gain them freedom from the senseless persecutions of demagogues. No public university could spend all of its time defending itself from the few elected officials who would not distinguish words from acts and who, in the fashion of the day, were threatening to punish people and institutions that allowed the full use of the First Amendment. And yet while it was necessary to disassociate the University from any hint of stigma, the administration had an obligation to the scholarly pursuit of truth; it could not abandon open forums without resigning its function.

The recruitment tables on the campus were banned, however. The one major exception was at Bancroft Way and Telegraph Avenue. There, the University allowed political action. Many administrators at the University thought that recruitment was possible on that strip of land because it belonged to the City of Berkeley rather than to the University.° Kerr knew otherwise; he had instructed the treasurer of the University to transfer the land to the city if possible. Other business interfered with the transfer, though. His instructions weren't carried out.

° The school, although public, is a corporation ruled by a Board of Regents resembling the councils of elders in the churches of the founders of the University. It is given "full powers of organization and government, subject only to such Legislative control as may be necessary to insure compliance with the terms of the endowments of the University and the security of its funds." There are 24 Regents; 16 are appointed by the Governor for terms of 16 years each and eight others, including the Governor himself, are public officials serving lesser terms as representatives of public interests—the lieutenant-governor, superintendent of schools, Speaker of the Assembly, president of the State Agricultural Board, president of the Alumni Association, president of the University, and president of the Mechanics Institute, which was begun in San Francisco after the gold rush to teach skills to unemployed miners. The Regents hold the University in their corporate name. Driven into the sidewalks around the campuses are plaques marking the beginning of their rule.

The controversial strip of land extends 26 x 60 feet in front of the Student Union Building. This structure was built in 1960–61 by the Associated Students of the University of California (ASUC), which is student operated but officially recognized and supported. (The ASUC was a voluntary organization until 1955, after which, in order to stabilize income and finance the construction of the new Student Union, whoever enrolled was compelled to join.) The University had helped the ASUC acquire land for the new building over a number of years, holding it in the name of the Regents as part of the campus and so extending its own boundaries beyond the historic border at Sather Gate, at the other end of the plaza. Therefore, many people at the University, as well as others in Berkeley, were confused about the ownership of the land.

I
THE ORIGINS OF DISCONTENT

While the Republican Convention was underway in San Francisco, a reporter for the Oakland *Tribune* visited the University of California in Berkeley to investigate a problem that had been raised by one of his editors. The assignment had a routine origin: the newspaper's city editor, Roy Grimm, had learned from its political writer that student Republicans favoring the candidacy of William Scranton for President were being recruited on the campus and that supporters of Barry Goldwater's candidacy were outnumbered there. The reporter, Carl Irving, ordinarily covered the campus with the help of the public affairs officer, Richard Hafner, Jr., and he went to see Hafner in the usual way.

Hafner wasn't in. Irving asked one of the assistants: Who owned the land on which recruitments were made, the University or the City of Berkeley? If the University was the owner, wasn't its Charter, which forbade political activity anywhere on its grounds, being violated?

These were difficult questions which the assistant preferred to check with higher authorities. They went to Hafner, who took them to the office of Edward Strong, Chancellor of the campus. Strong was in Hawaii (this was July, during the vacation period between semesters); the questions next went to Alex Sherriffs, Vice Chancellor. Sherriffs considered them carefully.

A committee of the University had been discussing whether or not the bicycles, tables, and crowds at Bancroft and Telegraph constituted a hazard. There was some talk about restricting the bicycles and some, too, though less, about limiting the number of tables. In any case, the issue was put aside until Irving's questions came in. At that time, a combination of events gave the University more to think about in its concern for the student safety on Bancroft. First, it was strenuously seeking the passage of a state bond issue for education in the coming election. Second, William F. Knowland, the editor and publisher of the *Tribune*, was the California manager of Barry Goldwater's campaign for the Presidential nomination. (In retrospect, Hafner and other members of the Administration rejected the widespread belief that the University reconsidered the question of the tables in response to political pressure from the *Tribune*, or even in the expectation of pressure. But all who were involved in the controversy agreed that the *Tribune* reporter's questions precipitated administrative action.)

The decision was made to ban the tables. Sherriffs signed a memorandum instructing Katherine A. Towle, Dean of Students, to apply a campus regulation forbidding political activity on campus. Dean Towle did not share this point of view. She said afterwards: "I considered the region too crowded, but the tables were harmless and useful as an escape valve." Nevertheless, she did her job and in conference with the students cited the formal policy of the Charter and Regents.

Kerr was away; Strong was unavailable; Towle was unable to debate issues. The decision was unanimous; the students had no appeal from it. The 18 organizations affected by the ruling petitioned for its reversal, urging that the University allow them full rights of assembly, advocacy, and speech. Dean Towle said she was bound to represent University policy.

The students became irascible—"both impudent and impertinent," Dean Towle said later. The students said it was their "duty to society" to persist in seeking the freedom of democratic action.

Soon afterwards—before the election—students recruited at Bancroft Way and Telegraph Avenue picketed the *Tribune* Building in Oakland. They carried signs urging Knowland to increase the number of Negroes being employed at his plant and asserted, through chants, speeches, and leaflets, that Knowland ruled the city while largely ignoring its Negro population, which comprises 23 per cent of its 370,000 people.

During the picketing, a group of nationalists carrying flags broke through the ranks of the students to comment on the efforts of civil rights workers.

While Knowland watched, the students and other civil rights pickets sat down in front of the driveway normally used by the *Tribune*'s circulation trucks. One student was injured during the arrests that followed; the police listened silently to the reaction of one of his friends. Then the arrests continued.

CHANCELLOR STRONG: *On the one side, an individual as a student is held responsible by the University for compliance with its rules and regulations. On the other side, when a student goes off-campus to participate in some social or political action, he goes so on his own responsibility as a citizen. He has no right, acting as a citizen, to involve the University, either by using its name or by using any of its facilities to further such action. For, were the University to become involved the consequence is clear. We ask and expect from the State an indispensable freedom residing in independence that rests on fulfillment of a public trust; namely, that the University will never allow itself to be dominated nor used by the parties, sects, or selfish interests. By honoring this public trust steadfastly, the University is enabled also to honor and defend the rights of its members to act freely in the public domain in the capacity as citizens. The consequence of defaulting on this public trust would be the erosion of the independence of the University and the destruction of the position maintained by the University respecting the responsibilities of an individual as a student in the University and respecting his rights and responsibilities as a citizen of the State.*

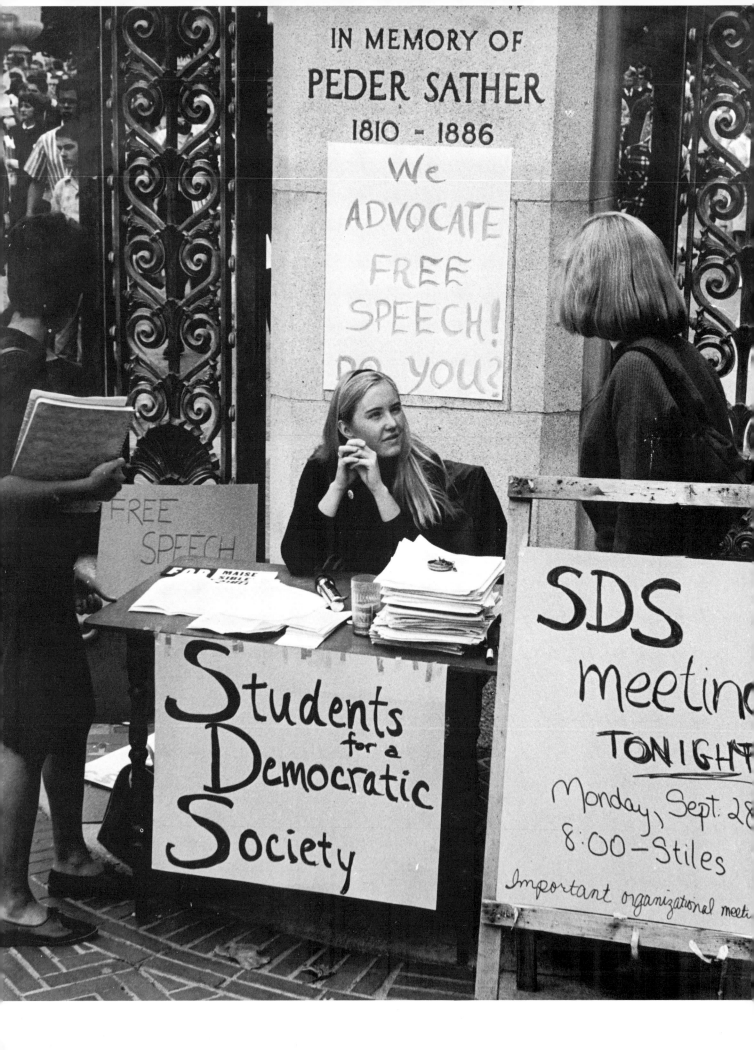

One evening, the groups forbidden to man the tables met and agreed to undertake direct action unless the University withdrew its regulation. They agreed on the methods being developed by civil rights workers: nonviolent action including vigils and rallies.

In this "United Front," the students met again with Dean Towle and were told that, while limited and licensed speech was acceptable under the University rules, "those who speak should be prepared to identify themselves as students or staff of the University." There could be no fund-raising, recruitment, or advocacy of controversial ideas under the regulations, she said.

The United Front* announced that action against the University would begin. A coed who helped to lead the group, Jackie Goldberg, said: "We don't want to be armchair intellectuals. For a hundred years people have talked and talked and done nothing. We want to help the students decide where they fit into the political spectrum and what they can do about their beliefs. We want to help build a better society." Then Clark Kerr said: "I don't think you have to have action to have intellectual opportunity. Their actions (the students)—collecting money and picketing —aren't high intellectual activity . . . It is not right to use the University as a basis from which people organize and undertake direct action in the surrounding community."

The United Front planned to break the University regulations, whatever the consequences, to force the issue. As 1,000 of their pickets organized to march on a University meeting, Chancellor Strong announced that the University would change its formerly adamant position and would permit students to distribute materials for political campaigns at nine separate regions, including the one at Bancroft Way and **Telegraph Avenue**. They could take positions for or against people

---

* Young Republicans, University Society of Individualists, Cal Students for Goldwater, California College Republicans, Particle Berkeley (student magazine), Young Democrats, Student Civil Liberties Union, Congress of Racial Equality (CORE), Friends of the Student Nonviolent Coordinating Committee (SNCC), Slate (campus political party), Students for a Democratic Society (SDS), W.E.B. DuBois Club, Young Socialist Alliance, Young People's Socialist League (YPSL), Independent Socialist Club (ISC), Women for Peace, Committee for Independent Political Action, May 2d Committee, and Students for Fair Housing.

Later groups sending delegates included the Interfaith Council, Democratic Socialist Club, and University Society of Libertarians.

or issues in the election (for the University itself was publicly supporting the bond issue for education); but the prohibitions against fund-raising, recruitment, and the advocacy of off-campus social and political action remained. To the students, the compromise seemed inadequate. Proceeding with their plan, they set up tables without permits and were confronted by campus faculty led by Arleigh Williams, Dean of Men. He instructed five students—Mark Bravo, Brian Turner, Donald Hatch, Elizabeth Gardiner Stapleton, and David Goins—to come to his office to be disciplined.

MARIO SAVIO: *Last summer I went to Mississippi to join the struggle there for civil rights. This fall I am engaged in another phase of the same struggle, this time in Berkeley, The two battlefields may seem quite different to some observers, but this is not the case. The same rights are at stake in both places—the right to participate as citizens in a democratic society and the right to due process of law. We are asking that our actions be judged by committees of our peers. We are asking that regulations ought to be considered as arrived at legitimately only from a consensus of the governed.*

That afternoon (September 30, 1964), 300 students appeared at Sproul Hall to see Williams, and 600 signed a statement claiming equal responsibility for manning the tables. Williams ordered the three leaders of this movement—Mario Savio, Arthur Goldberg, and Sandor Fuchs—to enter his office with the previously cited five. Again the 300 insisted on equal punishment. They were refused, and the united students waited outside the Dean's office until early morning. Supplied with food by friends outside the building, they spent the night quietly in the corridors of Sproul Hall, until at 2:40 a.m., after the eight were suspended indefinitely, they voted to leave the building. At the same time they announced that a "rally for free speech" would be held the next day.

Tables were set up again; and now police led by University deans came to take the names of the students behind them. The students waited, calm but defiant, as their names were taken. The issue at this point became twofold: the students' right to advocate, recruit, and raise funds for political reasons; and the University's insistence that the eight offending students be punished.

The Campus CORE table set up deliberately to violate the rules was manned by Jack Weinberg, a recent mathematics student who had become deeply engrossed in the civil rights movement. Weinberg refused to identify himself, and when he was arrested as a trespasser, he went limp and was carried to a police car.

The crowd was gathering for the Free Speech rally that noon (October 1, 1964). Seeing Weinberg's arrest, 100 students lay down in front of the police car and 80 lay down behind it; and all chanted: "Release him! Release him!" Mario Savio asked permission of the police to speak to the crowd from the top of the car. They gave it; he removed his shoes and spoke to several thousand students. Together this group held the police for 32 hours. Weinberg remained in the car and was fed through its windows, while on the roof Savio and others outlined the position of the students.

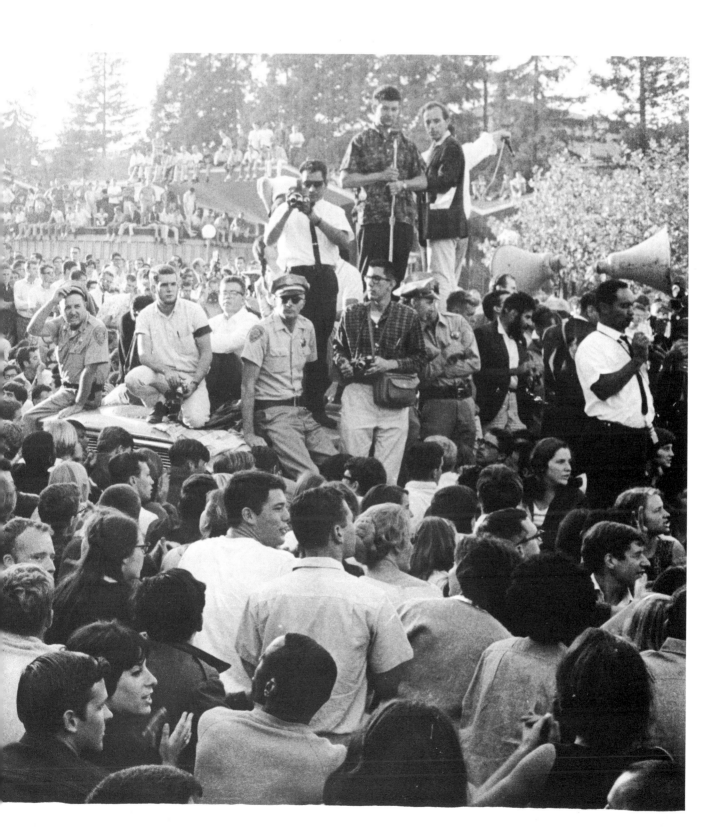

Charles Powell, president of the Associated Students of the University of California (Berkeley), was among the students who climbed to the top of the police car to speak. He was the official student leader and so was urged by the crowd to work beside Savio to negotiate for complete freedom of speech and the dismissal of charges against the eight students and Weinberg. Instead, Powell offered to put the issues to the Associated Student Senate. There was neither time nor ample student power for that, the audience indicated. Powell left.

Next, on Savio's advice, 150 students marched into Sproul Hall nearby, while 500 others remained to hold the car. By late afternoon more than 400 students were inside the hall, focusing on the office of the Dean of Students. Although the aisles were clear and it was possible to walk through Sproul Hall, many University employes in the building decided not to face the students and left that evening through windows.

While some faculty members tried to mediate between the Administration and the students that evening, police began to lock the doors of Sproul Hall. Two thousand students watched them; then 100 surged forward to begin a sit-in before the doors were closed. Twenty police retreated to a line at the main stairway; then the students gave up the sit-in and returned to the police car in which Weinberg was still prisoner. But the Administration issued an angry statement declaring that its discipline against the eight cited students was not negotiable. To this the United Front replied that direct action would continue. The students remained around the police car.

JACK WEINBERG: *These themes have been so well received because of the general feeling among the students that the University has made them anonymous; that they have very little control over their environment, over their future; that the University society is almost completely unresponsive to their individual needs. The students decry the lack of human contact, the lack of communication, the lack of dialogue that exists at the University. Many believe that much of their course work is irrelevant, that many of their most difficult assignments are merely tedious busy work with little or no educational value. All too often in his educational career, the student, in a pique of frustration, asks himself, "What's it all about?" In a flash of insight he sees the educational process as a gauntlet: undergraduate education appears to be a rite of endurance, a series of trials, which if successfully completed allows one to enter graduate school; and upon those who succeeded in completing the entire right of passage is bestowed the ceremonious title, Ph.D.*

By midnight (October 1–2, 1964) almost 2,500 demonstrators were in the plaza in front of Sproul Hall. Some were opposed to the United Front; as the demonstrators sang "We shall overcome!" Their antagonists, from the steps of the Hall, chanted "Mickey Mouse!" and threw lighted cigarettes and eggs into the crowd. There was no violence, however. The demonstrators refused to respond, and soon a Catholic Chaplain appealed for order and got it.

At one point more than 4,000 students surrounded the police car. Day and night the vigil went on, while religious leaders, then members of the faculty, tried to mediate between the Administration and the students. During this negotiation, Governor Brown, Kerr, and Strong agreed to call on local police to dissolve the crowd. By late afternoon the following day police took positions around the campus; they came from Berkeley, Oakland, Alameda County, and the California Highway Patrol. Five hundred patrolmen, many armed with riot sticks, occupied an area directly behind Sproul Hall. Meanwhile, the students and Administration worked out an armistice, one part of which was an agreement to attempt to deed the sidewalk at Bancroft Way and Telegraph Avenue to the City of Berkeley.

Savio agreed to address a rally of the FSM scheduled to be held in the plaza the next day. More than 7,000 students and faculty and staff members attended that meeting, covering the plaza and nearby balconies and rooftops. They were given instructions on how to be arrested: carry no sharp objects, take off rings and watches, loosen clothing, stay close together without linking arms, go limp. Students were told to give police only their names and addresses, to make no statements, and to ask for a lawyer.

But, it turned out, arrests might not be necesssary. At the scheduled time for Savio's speech he appeared before the crowd with the six-point agreement that had been negotiated between the Administration and students.

Savio climbed to the now flattened roof of the police car. He read the terms of the agreement. Then he said:

> *Let us agree by acclamation to accept this document. I ask you to rise quietly and with*
> *dignity and go home.*

The students left; police booked Weinberg; and Kerr held a press conference, during which he said: "Law and order have been restored without the use of force." But Strong, who was with Kerr at the conference, was silent. It became evident later that he thought Kerr weak for refusing to insist on punishment of the cited students.

On October 3–4, 1964, the United Front became the Free Speech Movement and appointed a nine-member Steering Committee to implement the agreement with the University.

CLARK KERR: *The president in the multiversity is leader, educator, creator, initiator, wielder of power, pump; he is also officeholder, caretaker, inheritor, consensus-seeker, persuader, bottleneck. But he is mostly a mediator.*

Hundreds of letters poured into the office of the Governor. They overwhelmingly supported the use of police to disperse the students. The Governor instructed Kerr to prepare a detailed report and Kerr, as well as Edward W. Carter, a Los Angeles department store executive and chairman of the Board of Regents, suggested that political extremists were responsible for the tension. Carter said: "It is regrettable that a relatively small number of students, together with certain off-campus agitators, should have precipitated so unfortunate an incident."

But a census later proved that the dissidents were unmistakably representative of most of the students on the campus, and that only a few non-students participated with them; these latter included some staff members and former students. Many people and groups supported the Free Speech Movement. The Northern California Chapter of the American Civil Liberties Union declared: "The ACLU does not share the opinion of the University Administration that the constitutional ban on political and sectarian activity is aimed at students." The Executive Committee of the Association of California State College Professors said: "Participation in social action, whether it is political or non-political, ought not only to be permitted, but actively encouraged, so long as it does not interfere with the regular instructional program. . . ."

Many professors were deeply moved by the risks taken by the students for the right of advocacy. Later during the controversy 14 of them were to issue this statement to the Academic Senate:

> *A great university should serve as a model for the free and unhampered exchange of ideas, for, by definition, it is an institution where men and women gather to ponder the things that matter most and to consider ways in which the human condition might be improved. . . . The orderly life of the university is threatened more by the proliferation of irritating and petty regulations than it is by the vigorous exchange of ideas or by the advocacy of causes.*

The uneasy peace prevailed. One thousand students assembled near the Student Union Building three days after the six-point agreement, and they heard their leaders insist that, by whatever means, the right to speech and advocacy on campus would be obtained. Professors John Leggett of Sociology and Charles Sellers of History addressed the students, too, and served to remind the students that they were not alone in their insistence on political action. Forty-three political science and economics teaching assistants issued a statement commending the rebels.

The students began a collection to pay for the damaged police car, the repair of which cost $334.30. No money was ever given to police, however.

II
THE NEEDS

New trouble developed almost immediately. Part of the six-point agreement created a Study Committee on Campus Political Activity to determine whether or not advocacy could be permitted on campus. Strong announced the appointments to this committee. The FSM protested that he had included only two of its spokesmen to the 12 member committee, and that he had violated that part of the agreement which permitted the Academic Senate, Administration, and students each to select part of the group.

Ten FSM spokesmen appeared at the first meeting of the committee and issued a statement which said: "As the duly elected representatives of the Free Speech Movement (FSM) we cannot in good conscience recognize the legitimacy of the present meeting." The committee ignored their protest. Kerr later defended the appointments as necessarily the responsibility of the administration alone.

Meanwhile, the Northern California Chapter of the American Civil Liberties Union notified the the University that it would defend the eight suspended students on the grounds that the University had violated political rights. Next, 650 members of 37 fraternities and sororities issued a petition declaring that FSM was "composed of responsible students" whom they supported. And the Academic Senate again passed a resolution favoring "maximum freedom for student political activity and the use of peaceful and orderly procedures in settling disputes," while adding that "force and violence have no place on this campus."

The FSM now needed these respectable counsellors; a large part of the press and public had begun to accuse it of quioxotically creating unreasonable pressures. And yet it persisted. Soon, the Ad Hoc Academic Senate Committee on Student Suspensions (known as the Heyman Committee for its chairman, Professor Ira Heyman of the School of Law), recommended that the eight suspended students be reinstated, for example, and when Chancellor Strong refused the FSM *Newsletter* announced: "We repeat: when the morass of mediation becomes too thick to see through, action must let in the light."

It became evident to the FSM that, because of the composition and tenor of the Campus Committee on Political Activity, no favorable decision could result in the question of advocacy. Therefore, 200 students resumed picketing on the Sproul Hall steps to protest abrogation of rights under the First and Fourteenth Amendments that they expected from the committee. To explain this gesture to its critics, the FSM issued a statement:

> *Although we continue to be a party to the Campus Committee on Political Activity, we feel that we must lift our self-imposed moratorium on political activity because the committee is already deadlocked over the issue of political advocacy and appears headed for a long series of radical disagreements. . . . We must exercise our rights so that the University is not permitted to deny us those rights for any long period, and so that our political organizations can function to their maximum capacity.*

Chancellor Strong accepted this challenge. He said, in an interview with the *Daily Californian:* "If the FSM returns to direct action tactics, this will constitute a clear breach of the agreement. . . . Students and organizations participating will be held responsible for their actions."

The FSM demonstrated again. Students set up the folding tables on the steps of Sproul Hall. They collected money and recruited others; they also advocated off-campus action—most emphatically, the support of the civil rights movement.

When University deans again took names (75, this time), the implacable students gave petitions demanding that they, too, be given responsibility for the defiance. Someone pulled an old dresser into the plaza. Speakers mounted it repeatedly to call for unified action against the inacceptable

regulations. Some of them represented the Graduate Coordinating Committee, which announced that it would join the FSM to set up tables whether or not they were suspended or arrested. (At a vote of the Graduate Coordinating Committee 220 graduate students agreed to man the tables; one said he would not.)

"FSM has abrogated the agreement of October 2," Kerr and Strong said in a joint statement, "and by reason of this abrogation the Committee on Campus Political Activity is dissolved. . . . Students participating in violation of rules will be subject to penalties through established procedures." In turn, the FSM accused the Administration of violating the agreement and declared that the dissolution of one more line of communication between the students and the Administration (that) makes the possibility of ultimate settlement even more remote."

Proceeding with its advocacy, recruiting, and fund-raising (in one case money for a haircut for a haircut for a professor), the FSM agreeably sent the names of the renegades to the Administration. All told, 832 names were on the final list: 75 who were cited, 220 graduate students and Teaching Assistants, and 607 undergraduates and additional graduates who volunteered.

At last the Heyman Committee reported its recommendations. They were to expunge the suspensions from the records of each cited student, and instead to "censure" each of them for a period of no more than six weeks. The committee noted that two of the eight students, Savio and Goldberg, were the leaders of picketing and sit-ins and therefore, it said, should be given more punishment than the others.

The Heyman Committee gave its opinion to the Academic Senate, of which it was part. Strong objected: the committee was appointed "to be advisory to me," he said. But he added that, since the opinion had been given to the Senate, he would await the Senate's action on it before responding himself.

The FSM observed this side debate between the faculty and Administration and appealed to the Regents for a chance to present its case. Its leaders were permitted to sit in the building where the Regents met, but not to speak there. Outside, during this appearance, a crowd of students gathered to hear how the Regents would react to the position of Kerr and Strong that the eight cited students be suspended. And the Regents at length reported an agreement. They supported their Administration on the issue of suspensions. Moreover, they announced an intention to permit "legal advocacy," which would have left them the right to define what was "illegal" and therefore with the power to prevent civil disobedience in the community. They voted to increase the campus police force and the personnel to discipline renegades.

This ignored the conclusions of the Heyman Committee, as well as its own hopes, the FSM declared. It called a mass rally, which was held and followed by a three-hour sit-in in Sproul Hall. On November 23, 1964, about two dozen members of the FSM started for the hall. They moved with resignation rather than with their former spirit, singing, in subdued voices, anti-Administration songs which had been put to Christmas carols. Three hundred students followed the first 24. But at 5 p.m., the FSM Steering Committee voted 6 to 5 to leave the building. Soon afterward, Sproul Hall was deserted.

The FSM declared a mass vigil at the time of the Regents' meeting in Berkeley, on November 20, 1964. Rallying on the steps of Sproul Hall, more than 5,000 of them heard Joan Baez, the folk-singer, sing and play songs of independence. Soon afterwards, most of these 5,000 marched to University Hall, the chief Administration building on the campus, where the Regents were meeting. They bore the massive sign: "Free Speech."

The street in the foreground is Bancroft Way. In the shadows at the lower left, where Telegraph Avenue ends, is the strip of land on which the "free speech" controversy arose. The Student Union Building is on the left. The circle above it is a fountain which has also been designated as an area for advocacy, and at the end of the mall is Sather Gate, which was an historical boundary of the University until the construction of the Student Union Building in 1960–61. Sproul Hall is the I-shaped building to the right of the picture's center. Police are stationed behind it, and at its entrance in the foreground paddy wagons are being held for students who are being taken prisoner.

III

DIRECT ACTION BEGINS

In letters to Savio, Goldberg, Jackie Goldberg, Brian Turner, and the 19 clubs which were members of the FSM, Chancellor Strong suddenly issued new charges which he said would require discipline. According to his letters, the newly cited students and clubs had "led and encouraged numerous demonstrators in keeping a University police car and an arrested person therein entrapped on the Berkeley campus for a period of approximately 32 hours, which arrested person the police were then endeavoring to transport to police headquarters for processing." Savio, in addition, was charged with organizing and leading demonstrators into Sproul Hall, "thereby blocking access to and from said office, disrupting the functions of that office and forcing personnel of that office to leave through a window and across a roof."

Strong declined to heed FSM demands that the new charges be dropped; even the Heyman Committee report (which recommended leniency) only covered the period up to September 30, he pointed out, and the incidents on which the new charges were based occurred afterwards. Before Strong's new efforts to discipline them, the FSM leaders had reached a critical point in their organization. The long negotiations had involved only a few of their members. Here, though, was a new issue. At UCLA, Santa Barbara, Riverside, Davis, and other University campuses there were demonstrations in behalf of the FSM.

The FSM offered the University 24 hours to withdraw the new actions. Unless it did so, the FSM said—with concurrence from the Graduate Coordinating Council—there would be a strike. In this ultimatum the FSM parted company with the ASUC, which announced, in a resolution, that the FSM's "present plans for civil disobedience are directed solely towards meaningless harrassment of the University."

There had been many attempts to reopen communications after the struggle over the police car; committees had been established by students, faculty, and Administration. However, after a full month of negotiation, the leaders of the FSM concluded, according to their *Newsletter*, that the Administration was not acting in "good faith," nor was it permitting them to share in whatever decisions were being made about the issues of advocacy and discipline. Therefore, the FSM decided to move against the University again.

MARIO SAVIO: *There is a time when the operation of the machine becomes so odious, makes you sick at heart, that you can't take part; you can't even tacitly take part, and you've got to put your bodies upon the gears and upon the wheels, upon the levers, upon all the apparatus and you've got to indicate to the people who run it, to the people who own it, that unless you're free, the machine will be prevented from working at all.*

On December 2, 1964, a student rally filled the plaza between the Student Union Building and Sproul Hall. Through this meeting it became evident that the members of the FSM and many who sympathized with it were committed to a new struggle with the Administration. The long negotiations were over; a new sit-in was to begin.

After formal speeches by FSM leaders Joan Baez, the folk-singer, spoke briefly. She said, echoing an aim of the civil rights movement:

"When you go in, go with love in your hearts."

The students filed quietly through the largely silent plaza into the hall as the voice of Miss Baez resonated above them:

"How many roads must a man walk down . . .

". . . before you call him a man?"

One thousand students filled Sproul Hall. When the first and second floors were totally occupied the newcomers moved into the third and fourth. They prepared for an occupation of two or three days.

That evening, the University police locked Sproul Hall as usual. Students were permitted to leave but not to enter. None did either through doorways—but food, and some students—were raised into the building at dusk and through the night.

Outside the building, students prepared signs through which they intended to close the campus. Inside, they established the "Free University of California." They created a study hall on one floor and held classes, under the direction of graduate students, on others. Their subjects included aesthetics, biology, anthropology, history and mathematics; one was called "The Nature of God and the Logarithmic Spiral." In a recreation area they showed films, including classics by Charlie Chaplin and Laurel and Hardy, or read or sang.

CHANCELLOR STRONG: *May I have your attention? I am Dr. Edward Strong Chancellor of the Berkeley Campus. I have an announcement.*

This assemblage has developed to such a point that the purpose and work of the University have been materially impaired. It is clear that there have been acts of disobedience and illegality which cannot be tolerated anywhere in our society.

The University has shown great restraint and patience in exercising its legitimate authority in order to allow every opportunity for expressing differing points of view. The University always stands ready to engage in the established and accepted procedures for resolving differences of opinion.

I request that each of you cease your participation in this unlawful assembly.

I urge you, both individually and collectively, to leave this area. I request that you immediately disperse. Failure to disperse will result in disciplinary action by the University.

Please go.

GOVERNOR BROWN: *I have tonight called upon law enforcement officials in Alameda County to arrest and take into custody all students and others who may be in violation of the law at Sproul Hall. I have directed the California Highway Patrol to lend all necessary assistance. These orders are to be carried out peacefully and quietly as a demonstration that the rule of law must be honored in California.*

I assume full responsibility for this in every shape, form, and manner. I felt it was the right thing to do. The overriding matter became one between the people of the State of California versus the demonstrators.

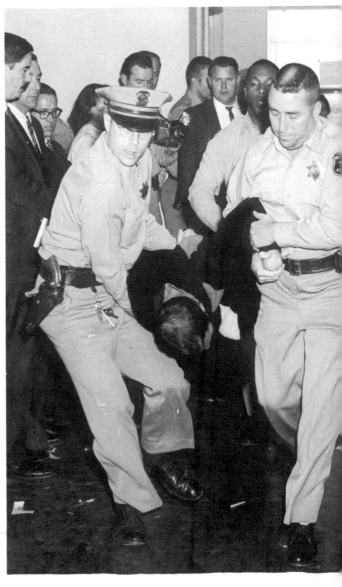

An FSM Leader: *Throughout the free speech controversy it has been evident that the Administration has assumed that the students would act as individuals who could be easily frightened away by a token exercise of authority. They expected that we would act with the same regard for precedent and pecking order that they had. The record has shown that we have acted more commendably.*

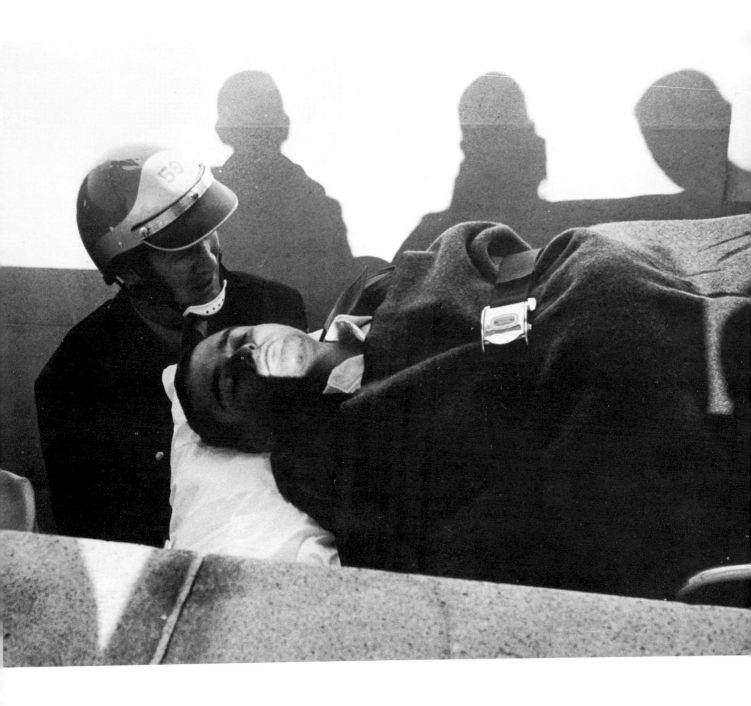

GOVERNOR BROWN (1961): *Far from discouraging your students' social and public interests, I propose that you positively exploit them.*

Here is an honorable source of college spirit; here is a worthy unifying and organizing principle for your whole campus life.

I say: thank God for the spectacle of students picketing—even when they are picketing me at Sacramento and I think they are wrong—for students protesting and freedom-riding, for students listening to society's dissidents, for students going out into the fields with our migratory workers, and for marching off to jail with our segregated Negroes.

At last we're getting somewhere. The colleges have become boot camps for citizenship—and citizen-leaders are marching out of them.

For a while, it will be hard on us administrators. Some students are going to be wrong and some people will deny them the right to make mistakes. Administrators will have to wade through the angry letters and colleges will lose some donations. We Governors will have to face indignant caravans and elected officials bent on dictating to state college faculties.

But let us stand up for our students and be proud of them.

If America is still on the way up, it will welcome this new impatient, critical crop of young gadflies. It will be fearful only of the complacent and passive.

THE EFFECTS OF REBELLION

The newspapers said that the trouble in Berkeley had generated the greatest mass arrest in the history of California. Six hundred and thirty-five policemen took more than 800 students into custody over a period of 12 hours. In the chilly darkness of a largely uninhabited, barren and rolling countryside, lines of cars miles long were parked on the normally busy highway in front of the Santa Rita Rehabilitation Center, 35 miles south of Berkeley. Most of the cars contained students, faculty members, or University personnel who, whether or not they were in sympathy with the arrested students, came to offer bail.

Throughout the country, educators reacted as though a sensitive nerve had been touched. A famous professor of philosophy, writing from his vantage point in New York City, set to work on a polemic against student irresponsibility. University presidents braced themselves for the responses on their own campuses. As leaders of the FSM toured other institutions, offering a message of rebellion against the Multiversity, thousands of dollars were raised to finance the rebels' progress. Artists, in one event, gave their work free to this cause. The sale of it raised more than $6,000.

On the Berkeley campus, the arrests led to a strike. Although Berkeley's professors largely condemned the arrests and strongly urged amnesty, as well as larger political freedom for the students, the state's and the university's administrations considered themselves agents, but not interpreters, of the law. Thus the stage was set for the collision of forces on the strange battleground which so much more often is dedicated to peaceful alternatives. Lectures stopped, study stopped, and the Multiversity paused. According to the *Daily Californian* more than half of the Teaching Assistants in anthropology, English, French, geography, German, history, Italian, molecular biology, philosophy, physics, political science, Slavic languages, social science, sociology, and Subject A (remedial English)—the "TA's" upon whom the University depends to function—refused to cross picket lines.

Someone at the University's Computer Center helped striking students bring IBM cards into their service. One bore a card which said:

"I am a UC student: Do Not Fold, Bend, or Mutilate."

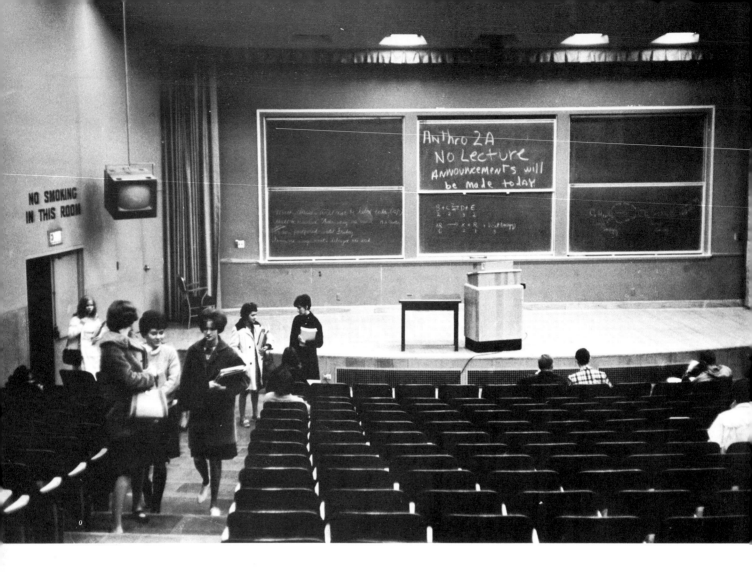

AN ASSOCIATE PROFESSOR OF PHILOSOPHY: *For me to teach would be a betrayal of those students who cannot be present.*

At a meeting of more than 5,000 students in the plaza FSM speakers, some of them recently discharged from jail, attacked the Multiversity in all of its aspects: the police, the state, and the administration. They announced that the general strike had completely closed the school. An FSM committee of more than 150 was at work calling on every University student for support. Based at a central headquarters, FSM patrols roamed the campus, radioing strike data to each other over walkie-talkies.

The "Free University of California" continued to function and to take enrollments. Graduate students and some specialists offered courses in it designed to give the students and teachers a closer relationship than the Multiversity could offer.

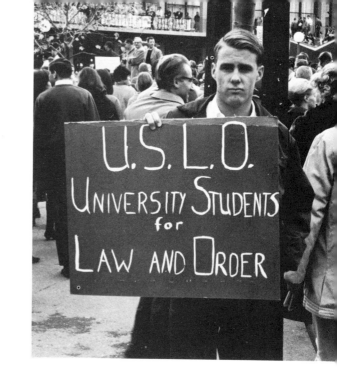

Kerr announced that the work of the University was being halted so that all of its members could gather for a meeting in the Greek Theatre, an open structure on campus which was modeled after the one at Epidaurus, where Sophocles was originally played. Chancellor Strong was absent. A public statement issued by the University said that he had been admitted to a hospital with abdominal pains. Later, the University urged him to resign, and he did.

A group called the Council of Department Chairmen had been formed to mediate between the Administration and students. At the meeting in the Greek Theatre, Kerr proposed to accept its suggestions. He told the students, faculty, and staff that "The University community shall abide by the new and liberalized political action rules and await the report of the Senate Committee on Academic Freedom." Kerr agreed with the chairmen that the sit-in and strike served "to obstruct rational and fair consideration of the grievances. . . ."

Before the meeting, Mario Savio had asked for permission to speak. The chairman of the meeting, Professor Robert Scalapino of the Political Science Department, had declined him permission on grounds that the meeting was "structured" in a form other than a debate. Savio said he was told that he could address the crowd briefly, with an announcement, when the meeting was adjourned. Accordingly, after the adjournment he moved to announce that the FSM would meet in the plaza immediately afterwards. Two University police seized him and dragged him behind the stage. His friends tried to rescue him, but were pushed aside. There was an outcry from the audience; violence seemed imminent. Then Savio was permitted to speak briefly.

MARIO SAVIO: *(To friends who crowded around him after the incident) Please leave here. Clear this disastrous scene and get down to discussing the issues.*

CLARK KERR: *(Later) There had been some indications of threats to disrupt the meeting. . . . The police were prepared. Apparently, they weren't aware the meeting was over. . . . Whether we have a new start seems doubtful.*

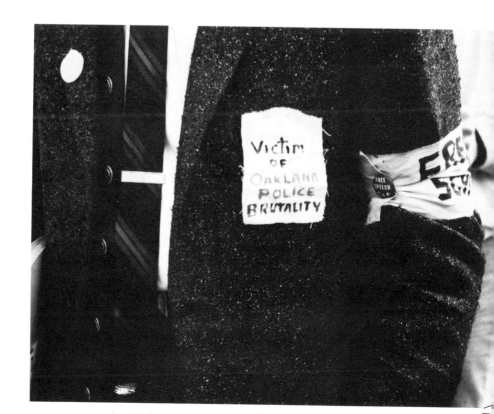

More than 10,000 attended the FSM meeting in the plaza. They heard their leaders say: "We are the ones who must save this University, but we're not going to save the University by capitulating." And: "The sit-in did not obstruct, but rather caused, the first rational discussion of the problem on campus."

The FSM Steering Committee had voted by that time to reject the proposal made by Kerr. This position, in the view of some FSM supporters, was a scorched earth policy, a pursuit of a goal of free speech while the University went up in flames. Moreover, the faculty regained some confidence in the Administration with the appointment of Martin Meyerson as Acting Chancellor (January 2, 1965). Meyerson gave a vigorous speech in which he indicated that the students were far from wholly wrong in all of their criticisms of the school.

But to a degree that would have been unbelievable a month earlier, the students had changed the entire structure of education at the University and perhaps, as a result, had affected teaching throughout the United States. In what the students regarded as complete understanding and support, the Berkeley Division of the Academic Senate, after a three-hour debate (December 8, 1964), had urged:

"1. That there shall be no University disciplinary measures against members or organizations of the University community for activities prior to December 8 connected with the current controversy over political speech and activity.

"2. That the time, place, and manner of conducting political activity on the campus shall be subject to reasonable regulations to prevent interference with the normal functions of the University; that the regulations now in effect for this purpose shall remain in effect provisionally pending a future report of the Committee on Academic Freedom concerning the minimal regulations necessary.

"3. That the content of speech or advocacy should not be restricted by the University. Off-campus political activities shall not be subject to University regulations. On-campus advocacy or organization of such activities shall be subject only to such limitations as may be imposed under Section 2.

"4. That future disciplinary measures in the area of political activity shall be determined by a committee appointed by and responsible to the Academic Senate.

"5. That the Division pledge unremitting effort to secure the adoption of the foregoing policies and call on all members of the University community to join with the faculty in its efforts to restore the University to its normal functions."

As the faculty left its meeting room, thousands of students applauded.

ADMISSION TO THIS MEETING IS RESTRICT
MEMBERS OF THE ACADEMIC SENATE, CONSIST
Regular INSTRUCTORS
Regular PROFESSORS
DEANS and DIRECTORS

ACTING AND VISITING PROFESSORS, LEC
AND TEACHING ASSISTANTS ARE NOT MEM

To help your colleagues at the door,
please identify yourself by name and tit

EPILOGUE

It appeared as though the drama had ended. It hadn't. The cases were pending against 773 students, who were represented by lawyers distinguished both for ability and for championing libertarian causes; the trial of the students became a matter of principle. The arrested students filed claims totalling $4.5 million, charging brutality by police and deprivation of rights. Moreover, students on other campuses had begun to take actions resembling those in Berkeley: 110 students at the University of Kansas had sat down in the office of the University president to gain a nondiscrimination clause in the regulations governing fraternities and sororities. At St. John's University there was a rally to reduce administrative censorship of the school newspaper.

After a long period in which the issues were debated and studied in committees and lawyers' offices a non-student unknown to the FSM altered the course of the University's history by sitting down on the campus with a sign using the slang for sexual intercourse. He was arrested, and three students (joined by five other non-students) who believed in free speech came to his defense. The nine were disowned by the FSM and attacked by every high public official from the Chancellor to the Governor. State Legislators, meanwhile, threatened to investigate the entire University and

to reduce its budget unless the offenders were punished. In Washington, D.C., the UnAmerican Activities Committee of the House of Representatives joined in the effort to rebuke the rebellious students. The committee's investigators had found that the Free Speech Movement contained children of leading American rebels. Five years before the controversy over speech and advocacy in Berkeley, students of the University had led an attack on the committee while it met in San Francisco, forcing it, through picketing which ended in mass arrests, to leave without concluding its hearings. Thus the committee regarded the FSM as a vehicle for the attitudes which had previously driven it from Northern California, and it held out the prospect of extended counter-actions.

Edward Carter, the Chairman of the Regents, demanded punishment for the offenders, too, but Kerr refused him on grounds that in doing so he would reopen the free speech controversy and would fail in his obligations to due process of law. Instead, Kerr and Chancellor Meyerson broke a new storm over Berkeley. They offered resignations, not to the Regents, but to the press. Reactions were obtained by the press, too, before the Regents could hear Kerr officially present his point of view. On every campus chancellors, faculties, and students voted overwhelmingly to ask Kerr to remain president of the University. Kerr's supporters among the Regents were thus well armed by the time of the meeting. The Governor led them. He insisted that due process of law be followed and that Kerr—who had still not officially submitted his resignation—be asked to remain. The Governor prevailed; both Kerr and Meyerson agreed to stay in office, and both were assured of new and greater strength.

Thus, if there were victories during the trouble in Berkeley, they were shared by all sides. Students gained a new consciousness of their own maturity and commitment to the cause of human dignity. Faculty gained a new awareness of how far circumstances had drawn it from the common defense of academic freedom. The Administration had been shown how impersonal it had become. The people, perhaps, were aroused sufficiently to think about the sea of ambiguities into which modern society is drifting.

True, the University had shed some blood. But that is the stuff with which the tree of liberty is watered.

CREDITS

The principal photographers for *The Trouble in Berkeley* were George Crow, Ronald Enfield, Howard Harawitz, Helen Nestor, and Douglas Wachter. The pages on which their work appears, as well as the work of others, are:

Special credit is owed to Robert Yamada, manager of the Books Unlimited Cooperative, Inc., of Berkeley, who, during the course of the events which are chronicled in *The Trouble in Berkeley* first suggested the importance of their being told in a book.